BIG BO

YouTube

Adam Sutherland

First published in paperback in 2015 by Wayland
Copyright © Wayland 2015

Dewey categorisation: 338.7'61-dc23

ISBN: 978 0 7502 8921 4

Libraray Ebook ISBN: 978 0 7502 8530 8

10 9 8 7 6 5 4 3 2 1

Commissioning editor: Annabel Stones
Designer: LittleRedAnt (Anthony Hannant)
Picture researcher: Shelley Noronha

Wayland is an imprint of Hachette Children's Group
Part of Hodder & Stoughton
Carmelite House, 50 Victoria Embankment
London EC4Y 0DZ

Printed in Malaysia

An Hachette UK company
www.hachette.co.uk
www.hachettechildrens.co.uk

Picture acknowledgements: The author and publisher would like to thank the following
for allowing their pictures to be reproduced in this publication.
Cover: Eric Carr/Alamy; title page: iStock Images: p.4: Netphotos/Alamy; p.5: White House Photo/
Alamy; p.6: YouTube/Photoshot; p.7: Rex Features; p.8: UPPA/Photoshot; p.9: CTK/Alamy; p.11,
top: Shutterstock; p.11, bottom: AFP/Getty Images; p.12, top: Jeff Morgan 02/Alamy; p.12, bottom:
Picture Alliance/Photoshot; p.14: YouTube/Photoshot; p.15 WireImage/Getty; p.16 & 21: CTK/Alamy;
p.17: Stefan Chabluk Illustration; p.18: Shutterstock; p.19: Shutterstock; p.20: AFP/Getty Images;
p.21: Paul Kitagaki Jr/Sacramento Bee/MCT/Photoshot; p.22 YouTube/Photoshot; p.23 YouTube/
Photoshot; p.24 Juliane Thiere/Alamy; p.25: Getty Images for YouTube; p.26: Photoshot; p.27:
Keith Morris/Alamy.

Contents

It's a YouTube world

It's November 2013, and YouTube is streaming its first Music Awards live from New York City. With 60 million votes cast, and appearances on the night from global superstars Lady Gaga, Eminem and Taylor Swift, it could soon become as important an event in the music calendar as MTV's Video Music Awards. What next, a show to rival the Oscars?

YouTube's presence is all around us – and still growing. At the time of writing, the world's largest video streaming website attracts 800 million visitors every month, with over 72 hours of video uploaded every minute. By the time you read this, those figures will be even larger!

So how did the brainchild of three twentysomethings, launched from above a pizza restaurant in San Mateo, California, become not only the third most popular website in the world, but also such a unique source of entertainment, as well as an important social, and at times political, tool?

What started as a website for viral videos of singing cats is today believed to be the future of entertainment. Unlike television, YouTube allows you to watch what you want, when you want – finding content either through searches or social media recommendations.

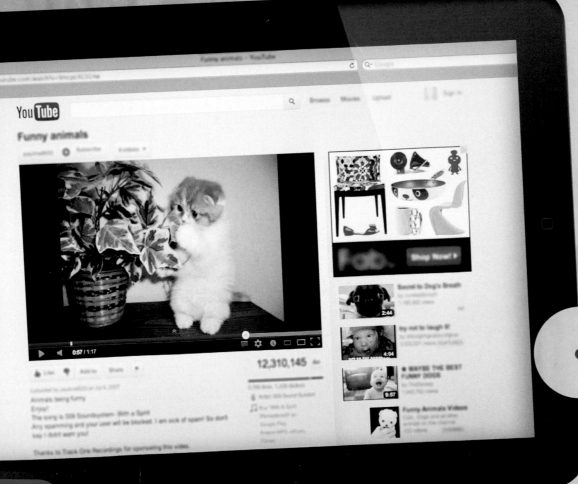

YouTube was originally a source of cute, entertaining, user-generated content.

Just as importantly, YouTube channels have the ability to interact directly with their audience, take on board comments and tailor their content – practically in real time.

'The ability to interact with their audience is a critical part of [the channels'] success,' says Sara Mormino, director of YouTube content operations in Europe, the Middle East and Africa (EMEA). 'It's a two-way dialogue that was not possible with traditional media.'

Over the next pages, we look at the YouTube phenomenon – from its launch, growth, purchase by Google, and continued growth and huge financial losses – to the YouTube we know today. Enjoy the ride!

President Obama takes part in a online interview with YouTube from the White House in December 2012.

YouTube's march into the record books

"Our community plays a vital role in ... YouTube ... that change media"

Chad Hurley, 2006, Google press release on the purchase of YouTube

YouTube Today

800 Million+
monthly unique visitors

More than the total population of Europe

72 Hours+
video uploaded per minute

More than a decade of content every day

One Million+
partner program members

More than the total population of Delaware

No.2 Search Engine

Larger than Bing, Yahoo, Ask and AOL added together

Four Billion
hours of video viewed each month
More than 450,000 years of video every month

It's good to share

Ground-breaking ideas can often come from the simplest of sources. In the case of YouTube – the world's number one website for uploading, viewing and sharing videos – it began with a party for three workmates in San Francisco.

At the start of 2005, Chad Hurley, Steve Chen and Jawed Karim – all former employees of the secure web payment site Paypal – were having a dinner party. As the story goes, the trio were unable to find a way to quickly and simply share video clips after the event due to restrictions on the size of email attachments, and YouTube was born.

Chen has since commented that the birth of YouTube has been simplified 'for marketing purposes'. What we do know for sure is that the domain name www.youtube.com was activated on 14 February 2005 and the first video, a 19-second clip entitled 'Me at the zoo' featuring co-founder Jawed Karim, was uploaded on 23 April of the same year.

Jawed Karim at the zoo – YouTube's first ever clip!

An early YouTube homepage from 2006.

The site was opened to the public in a 'beta' (testing) version in May 2005, six months before the official launch in November. The new company attracted investment of $3.5m (£2.1m) from venture capital firm Sequoia Capital. As well as money, they gained business expertise with Roelof Botha, former chief financial officer of Paypal, who joined the YouTube board of directors. In April 2006, Sequoia and fellow investment firm Artis Capital Management put a further $8m (£5m) into the business.

The money was spent on computing power – the huge network of servers that stores uploaded videos, and allows visitors to stream them smoothly and quickly. The site was a huge hit. By June 2006 more than 65,000 new videos were being uploaded, and the site was receiving 100 million video views every day.

Business Matters

Forming a company

A 'limited' or 'incorporated' company is a business owned by shareholders (people who own shares in the company), and run by directors. The company's shares have a basic value, for example £1 each, which stays the same, and a 'market value', which goes up and down depending on how good an investment the shares are judged to be by people outside the company who want to buy them.

Brains

Behind The Brand

Chad Hurley
YouTube co-founder and former CEO

As CEO of YouTube, Hurley oversaw the company's growth from a start-up to the world's third most visited website. Until he stepped down as CEO in October 2010, his role was overseeing the growth of the brand, and the transition into profit through advertising revenues.

Hurley has a BA in Fine Arts from Indiana University of Pennsylvania, and was hired as PayPal's first graphic designer. He created its official logo during his job interview!

In 2013, Hurley launched MixBit, a Smartphone video-editing app, with YouTube co-founder Steve Chen through their company AVOS Systems.

Along comes Google

Within a year of its launch, YouTube was ranked the fifth most popular site on the Internet. In the 12 months to August 2006, site visits had soared from 2.8 million to 72 million per month.

YouTube had become an Internet phenomenon. It was easy to use – you could watch videos on the site without downloading any special software, or even registering. And everything was there! If you wanted to see a clip of England winning the 1966 World Cup, or Lady Gaga wearing a dress made of meat at the Video Music Awards, they were both there, along with countless clips of weird, funny, informative and other cool stuff that site visitors loved.

The Queen uploading a video to YouTube's Royal Channel in 2008, during a visit to Google HQ in London.

> **"** The YouTube team has built an exciting and powerful media platform that complements Google's mission to organize the world's information and make it universally accessible and useful. **"**

Google chief executive Eric Schmidt, 2006, Google press release on the purchase of YouTube

Business Matters

The Google empire, including YouTube, Chrome, Google + and Gmail.

The Unique Selling Point (USP)

A USP is the unique quality about a company's product or service that will attract customers to use or buy it rather than an alternative product from a competitor. YouTube stood out from competitors because, according to co-founder Jawed Karim, it is a site 'where anyone could upload content that everyone else could view... Up until that point, it was always the people who owned the website who would provide the content'.

In October, Google announced that it was buying YouTube for $1.65bn (£1.1bn).

Why? Advertisers love sites like YouTube that not only attract large amounts of traffic, but also have the potential to hold visitors for extended periods of time.

Google calculated that even if just 10 per cent of the $54bn (£33bn) spent annually on TV advertising made the shift to video sites like YouTube, then $1.65bn was a small price to pay for the income they could potentially earn.

According to Chad Hurley, YouTube decided to sell because they lacked the resources to cope with the site's extraordinary growth. 'When we started, we thought one million daily uploads would be great,' he remembers. Instead, they were getting a hundred times that many. 'We thought we'd burn up our bandwidth. We worried our servers would go down.'

At that time, YouTube was making no money, so the deal with Google meant financial investment, more servers and computers, more brainpower, and more help finding broadcast partners and figuring out how to place advertising on the site.

Millionaires overnight

Google's purchase of YouTube gave the owners shares in the search giant that were worth many millions of pounds!

Artis Capital Management $783m (£486m)

Sequoia Capital $446m (£277m)

Chad Hurley $395m (£245m)

Steve Chen $326m (£202m)

Jawed Karim $64m (£39m)

Content is king – as long as it's legal

By 2007 YouTube was becoming part of the mainstream – 7 of the 16 US Presidential candidates announced their campaigns on the site! It also set about gaining traditional broadcasters' confidence by tackling piracy and signing important content licensing deals.

Winning the support of the global entertainment industry was YouTube's biggest challenge. Many of its video clips were taken from films, TV shows or sporting events and uploaded to the site without the knowledge or permission of the broadcaster. Although YouTube offered to remove all offending videos when it received a complaint from the copyright holder, this was still a potential area of conflict – and costly lawsuits – that Google was keen to avoid.

YouTube and Google jointly announced a series of new distribution deals. Universal Music Group signed a deal protecting the rights of its label's artists, and US TV channel CBS signed a deal offering short video clips like news, sport and entertainment on the site. In turn, the CBS Videos YouTube channel earned CBS a share of advertising revenues.

YouTube also launched a content-management programme – Content ID – that alerted copyright holders automatically when any part of their content was uploaded. Copyright holders then had the option to remove it, sell ads against it, or use it as a promotional tool. Today, Content ID generates a third of YouTube's income.

In November 2008, YouTube signed further agreements with MGM, Lion's Gate and CBS, allowing all three to post full-length films and TV episodes on the site, accompanied by ads, in a section of the US website called 'Shows'. In November 2009, a version of 'Shows' was launched for UK viewers offering around 4,000 full-length shows from more than 60 partners.

The move helped YouTube keep growing in popularity. By 2010, it was ranked as the third most visited site on the Internet, behind Google and Facebook.

Business Matters

Branding

All the qualities and features of a product, including its name and its appearance, are presented to the customer as a brand. To be successful, all brands — from YouTube to McDonalds to Nike — need to be distinctive (stand out in some way from competitors), consistent (always provide the same level of quality, and therefore be seen as reliable), recognizable (through a logo or 'look' of a product) and attractive. The simple black and red YouTube logo has become as recognizable as a Nike swoosh or the McDonalds golden arches.

Brains
Behind The Brand

Steve Chen
co-founder of YouTube

Chen was born in Taiwan and moved to the USA with his family at eight years old. He studied computer science at the University of Illinois, but left before graduating to join PayPal as one of its first employees.

At YouTube, Chen was the company's chief technology officer. His role was to keep the site running smoothly, and quickly react to problems as they arose. Chen was a fellow employee of Chad Hurley's at PayPal, and helped PayPal launch in China. He is also a former employee of Facebook. He now co-owns AVOS Systems with Hurley.

YouTube's co-founders Chad Hurley and Steve Chen. The pair are still working together on new projects.

US Presidential candidates on stage in 2007, taking part in a debate broadcast live on YouTube.

YouTube in trouble

YouTube experienced huge growth and global brand awareness. It captured 43 per cent of the US online video market, and had 14 billion video views per month – but it still wasn't making money.

Two years into the program, YouTube was earning roughly $240m (£150m) in ad revenue. Unfortunately, its operating costs (computers, bandwidth, staff, office space and so on) cost an estimated $710m (£440m). That's a loss of over $470m (£290m)!

The problem was that there was far more user-generated content on the site than professionally produced material. This content was harder to monetize as advertisers prefer to run clips at the start of more popular films and TV shows. At the same time, this content added significantly to the costs of running the site, specifically in terms of bandwidth (the amount of computing power required to store the videos and stream them to site visitors).

Advertisers, such as Hyundai, have increasingly turned to YouTube and away from traditional print media.

In May 2007 YouTube launched its Partner Program, a system based on Google's AdSense advertising system, which allows the person who uploaded the video to share in the revenue produced by advertising on the site. YouTube takes 45% of the revenue with the other 55% going to the uploader.

YouTube's Partner Program has helped turn the slogan 'Broadcast Youself' into big money for many YouTubers.

YouTube had a number of choices: it could refocus the site on professionally produced content with existing customer loyalty and real monetization prospects, for example network TV shows; it could put its efforts into promotional partnerships with big-name brands like Nike, Toyota and Disney-Pixar; or it could adopt a subscription model, either charging people to view certain members-only content, or requiring users to create a paid account to be able to upload videos. All of these, however, were against the spirit of the site.

How would YouTube turn loss into profit, and keep its identity?

Brains

Behind The Brand

Jawed Karim
co-founder of YouTube

Karim was born in Germany but moved to the USA with his parents – both scientists – at 12 years old. Along with Steve Chen, he studied computer science at the University of Illinois but left before graduating to join PayPal. Much of PayPal's security software, including its anti-fraud protection, was designed by Karim.

When YouTube was sold to Google in 2006, Karim continued working part-time as an advisor, but went back to university to study computer science at Stanford University. In 2008, he launched a venture capital fund, Youniversity Ventures, to help students develop and launch their own businesses.

Business Matters

Profit and loss

A profit and loss statement is a company's financial report that indicates how the revenue (money received from the sale of products and services before expenses are taken out, also known as the 'top line') is transformed into the net income (the result after all revenues and expenses have been accounted for, also known as the 'bottom line'). It shows the revenues for a specific period, and the cost and expenses charged against those revenues. The purpose of the profit and loss statement is to show company managers and investors whether the company made or lost money during the period being reported.

The power of partners

Advertising had been Google's path to profit, and they were convinced they could do the same for YouTube.

Google's first step was moving Salar Kamangar from parent company Google over to YouTube. Kamangar had been one of the creator's of Google's hugely profitable advertising system – charging advertisers for every thousand views (known as CPMs).

Kamangar began to harness the power of YouTube's Partner Program to create a generation of 'bedroom' YouTube stars (see page 18–19). By selling advertising on popular homegrown channels, the site generated monthly revenue for its 30,000 partners. The top 500 partners now earn close to £100,000 per year!

> ❝ We're going to see tens of thousands of channels that are able to find their audience and build content specifically for that audience. ❞

Ben McOwen Wilson, director of content partnerships, YouTube

Tanya Burr's YouTube channel now has over 1.3 million subscribers.

Tanya Burr ♡

tanyaburr.co.uk

1,348,323

Next, Kamangar recruited Robert Kyncl (see biography on page 21). Kyncl pioneered web streaming of video at Netflix, striking deals with Hollywood studios to license its content online and generating huge profits for the company. At first, Kyncl concentrated on strengthening YouTube's own movie-streaming business. This met with limited success, however as many studios were already tied into long-term licensing deals with companies like Netflix.

Kyncl and Kamangar's next move was more ambitious: to turn YouTube into the world's number one resource for high-quality, studio-produced TV shows – 'webisodes' lasting between 4-10 minutes.

The idea was to recruit programme makers, offering $100m (£62m) in funding (advances against projected advertising revenues), and launching around 100 original channels. YouTube would have exclusive rights to stream the shows for one year, but apart from selling advertising, it would not invest in the promotion or marketing of the shows in the way that traditional TV channels do.

Among the first channels to launch were Life and Times, focusing on the interests of rapper Jay-Z; skateboard channel RIDE from champion skater Tony Hawk; and news and comedy channels from The Wall Street Journal and The Onion.

Today, those channels have multiplied and are watched by millions of subscribers.

Skateboarder Tony Hawk now has his own YouTube channel, RIDE.

Three webisodes to watch now

WIGS
Short films and documentaries about the lives of women. Actress Anna Paquin from the *True Blood* series is one of the stars.
Average length: 7 mins
Subscribers: 257,000

All about the McKenzies
A British comedy likened to *The fresh prince of Bel Air*, with Samuel McKenzie dreaming of becoming a Hollywood acting legend.
Average length: 4 mins
Subscribers: 1,700

The Khan Academy
Offers 'a free world-class education for everyone'. Subjects include maths, computer programming and history.
Average length: 4 mins
Subscribers: 1.4m (million)

YouTube goes global

Like its parent company Google, YouTube was focused on worldwide expansion, which opened up a massive global market of viewers – and advertisers.

In June 2007 Google CEO Eric Schmidt launched YouTube's new 'localization' system. Localization is a way of adapting computer software to specific regions or languages, for example the Basque dialect in France, or Catalan in Spain, by adding certain location-specific components, and translating text.

During June of that year, nine local YouTube channels launched, including Brazil, Japan, UK, Spain, France and Italy. Eight more followed before the end of the year, including Australia, New Zealand, Canada (with English and French versions), Germany and Russia. By the end of August 2013, there were over 50 different language versions of the site, covering North and South America, Europe, the Middle East and Australasia.

The Czech language edition of YouTube, launched in October 2008.

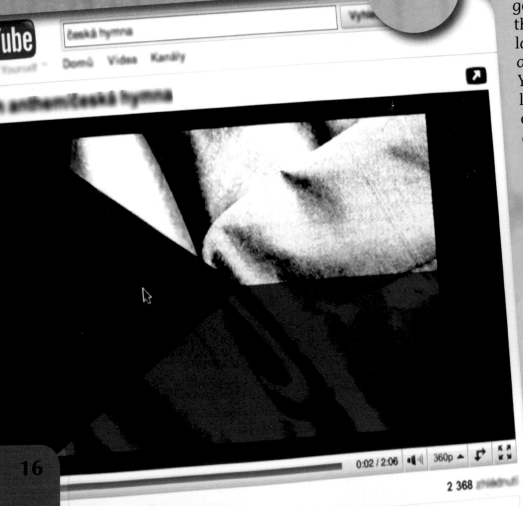

The global expansion hugely increased YouTube's ability to generate advertising revenue through the site. Not only could large international brands now advertise on a global scale, but YouTube could also tap into lucrative national markets. In other words, viewers would always see advertising that was relevant to them whatever country they lived in.

However, YouTube's global reach has often been affected by censorship in certain countries, either on a temporary or permanent basis. At the time of writing, YouTube is permanently banned in China, Iran, Pakistan and Turkmenistan. More often, YouTube is banned temporarily if a country's government reacts angrily to content posted on the site.

For example, YouTube was banned in Libya in January 2010 when it featured videos of demonstrations by families of detainees killed in Abu Salim prison. It was reinstated at the end of 2011 after the Libyan Civil War.

Because of YouTube's global accessibility and massive number of users, its impact has grown from an entertainment site to a valuable tool in countries fighting for democracy. It can provide a broadcasting outlet for protest groups – a voice for people struggling to be heard. In that way, it is invaluable.

YouTube's global censorship

Business Matters

Expansion

This means increasing the size of a company, or the scale of its operations. In YouTube's case, this happened when they expanded beyond the US, so that eventually everyone in the world could use it. Expansion can make a business more profitable as well as more 'cost efficient', by increasing profits at a rate faster than costs.

Afghanistan
Turkmenistan
Tajikistan
Germany
UK
Russia
Armenia
Turkey
Tunisia
Syria
Iran
China
Morocco
US
Libya
Bangladesh
Thailand
Sudan
UAE
Pakistan
Malaysia
Indonesia
Brazil

Permanently blocked
Temporarily blocked

YouTube superstars

The YouTube Partners Program has created a generation of YouTube superstars! Here we meet three of them.

Jamal Edwards, SB.TV
350,000 subscribers

At 14 years old, Londoner Jamal Edwards started recording videos of foxes raiding the dustbins outside the tower block where he lived. By 15 he was following the grime music scene, filming rappers performing for his Smokey Barz TV channel.

In 2009, Edwards persuaded YouTube to make him an official partner, and today the 22 year old has interviewed Prime Minister David Cameron, is credited by music artists Jessie J and Rita Ora as helping to launch their careers, and is worth an estimated £8m!

Edwards puts his success down to hard work and ambition. 'I was always trying to expand. I could have just stayed in West London, but [I went] east, north, south, central! I was uploading a video every day. I'd finish college, and I'd be editing my videos on the way home [to get] my clip online first.'

YouTuber Jamal Edwards at London Fashion Week 2013.

Tanya Burr's fans now look for style tips as well as make-up tips from her YouTube channel.

Tanya Burr
550,000 subscribers

Norfolk-born Burr left school at 16, did a short make-up course, and started work on the beauty counter of her local department store. When she got home, she would post step-by-step make-up tutorials on YouTube. 'Early on, they were mainly celebrities' looks,' she says. 'How to recreate famous faces.'

Two years later, Burr left her job to devote herself to her blog and tutorials full time. Like fellow YouTuber Zoella, Burr's influence over fans' buying habits has made her an important ally to fashion brands. A Mulberry handbag she featured in one video caused the Mulberry website to be bombarded with hits, and resulted in an invite for Burr to the Mulberry show at London Fashion Week. But Burr keeps her feet on the ground. 'The most important thing is to give viewers what they want and to keep the videos unique and professional.'

Charlie McDonnell, Charlieiscoollike
2.2m subscribers

McDonnell started posted videos from his home in Bath in April 2007 at the age of 16. One of his earliest videos 'How To Get Featured on YouTube' made it onto YouTube UK's homepage and saw his subscribers jump from 150 to 4,000 in just two days.

In January 2008, to celebrate reaching 25,000 subscribers he asked for challenge suggestions from viewers. He completed 25 videos, including a suggestion that came from TV presenter Philip Schofield and his daughter: to perform the 'Hoedown Throwdown' dance from the film *Hannah Montana: The Movie.*

In June 2011, McDonnell became the first UK YouTuber to reach one million subscribers. His videos now end with a voiceover from *QI* presenter Stephen Fry telling viewers they are honorary 'coollikes' for watching Charlie!

Behind the scenes at YouTube HQ

What's it like working at the heart of one of the most successful Internet companies in the world? We go behind the scenes at YouTube's California offices to find out.

Like the best companies in Silicon Valley, YouTube strives to find the very best talents and keep them from leaving. One way they do that is making employees' working lives as fun, entertaining and full of perks as possible.

If you're lucky enough to be one of the 550 employees working at YouTube's San Bruno headquarters, you can start your day by hopping onto one of the company's air-conditioned – and free – buses running in and out of San Francisco. Relax and forget about the rush hour traffic. In fact, bring your pet – many YouTubers bring their dogs to work with them every day.

When you arrive, grab a bike or a scooter – they're also provided free – and find your way to your desk. No gloomy workspaces here, everything is open-plan and well-designed with large windows to let in as much natural light as possible. In keeping with the green credentials, all work benches scattered around the office are made from eucalyptus grown on site.

The putting green at YouTube HQ – a good way to blow off steam!

At lunchtime, sit down for a healthy – and free! – lunch prepared by award-winning San Francisco chef Trent Page. If you're feeling a little drowsy on the way back to your desk, how about some downtime in one of the 'nap pods' spread around campus?

Business Matters

Human Resources

The Human Resources (HR) department of a company is responsible for putting in place and maintaining the business practices that allow effective people management. Some key responsibilities of an HR department are: 1) training; 2) staff appraisal: a formal process, performed by managers on their staff, which aims to communicate how they are performing and to discuss what they need in order to improve and develop; 3) staff development: the processes in the company designed to identify the people with potential, keep them in the organisation, and move them into the right positions.

Or if you're feeling more energetic, how about 15 minutes on the putting green – yes, it's inside the office, and a great spot for brainstorming!

In the afternoon, as you head to a meeting with co-workers in one of the conference rooms named after popular video games, don't bother with the lift, use the slide – in YouTube red – to quickly take you down from the third to the second floor.

Who said work can't be fun?

YouTube employees can take the slide between floors – in YouTube red of course.

Brains

Behind The Brand

Robert Kyncl
Global Head of Content

Czech Republic-born Kyncl oversees YouTube's business functions such as content, sales, marketing and operations. It is his job to extend YouTube into a specialized multi-channel environment.

Kyncl joined YouTube in 2010 from Netflix, where he was Vice President of Content Acquisitions and in charge of company acquisitions for streaming TV shows and movies over the Internet.

YouTube's greatest hits

What have been the most popular videos on YouTube? Here we list the ten most popular videos ever, and investigate landmarks in YouTube's video history.

A history in video

April 2005 YouTube co-founder Jawed Karim posts , 'Me at the zoo' – the first video on the site.

October 2005 Nike promotional video featuring footballer Ronaldinho is the first one million-hit clip.

December 2005 US comedy show *Saturday Night Live* airs 'Lazy Sunday' clip featuring comedian Andy Samberg, increasing YouTube traffic by 83%.

April 2006 'The Evolution of Dance', a 6-minute clip featuring 50 years of dance crazes, becomes the most popular clip in YouTube history with 131 million views.

May 2008 13 hours of video uploaded every minute.

January 2009 President Obama launches his own YouTube channel. The Pope launches his own YouTube channel. Live streaming of U2 concert.

March 2010 24 hours of video uploaded every minute.

April 2011 YouTube Live launches – providing live streaming of everything from the Royal wedding to the Olympics.

Feb 2013 72 hours of video uploaded every minute.

From the first clip uploaded, Jawed Karim's 'Me at the zoo' (see page 6) to PSY's *Gangnam Style* – the most viewed video on YouTube, with over 1.7 billion views to date – YouTube has seen phenomenal growth. The growth has not just been in the amount of videos uploaded, and the number of people watching, but in the changing content from user-generated to mainstream music videos and network programming.

Business Matters

Critical mass

This is when a company expands until it achieves a strength or dominance in any particular market (or in YouTube's case, country) that means it achieves automatic brand recognition and can effectively control the market.

A clip from PSY's Gangnam Style – the video was a massive hit on YouTube.

Brains

Behind The Brand

Salar Kamangar
CEO of YouTube

CEO Salar Kamangar has helped turn YouTube's loss into profit.

Kamangar replaced Chad Hurley as YouTube CEO in 2010. The ninth employee to join Google, Kamangar wrote the company's first business plan, and was responsible for its legal and financial departments, before becoming a founder member of its product team.

Before taking over at YouTube, Kamangar was Vice President of Google's Web Applications. He has a degree in Biological Sciences from Stanford University.

YouTube's ten most popular videos*

Rank	Video	Uploaded on	Number of views*
1	Gangnam style by PSY	July 2012	1.8bn
2	Baby by Justin Beiber	9 Feb 2010	922m
3	On the floor by Jennifer Lopez	3 March 2010	700m
4	Love the way you lie by Rihanna	5 Aug 2010	614m
5	'Charlie bit my finger – again!'	22 May 2007	590m
6	Party Rock Anthem by LMFAO	8 March 2011	587m
7	Gentleman by PSY	13 April 2013	575m
8	Waka Waka by Shakira	4 June 2010	566m
9	Bad Romance by Lady Gaga	23 Nov 2009	544m
10	Ai Se Eu Te Peg by Michel Teló	25 Jul 2011	532m

* Correct to October 2013

YouTube's political and social uses

In August 2013 chemical attacks on Syrian civilians left an estimated 1,400 people dead. British MPs were recalled from their summer break to view a report by the Joint Intelligence Committee, and decide what action to take in response to the attacks. As part of their decision process, they viewed a series of YouTube videos – watched over one million times – that formed the backbone of the report.

YouTube is no longer just an entertainment service. As we saw from the countries that censor YouTube (p16-17) the site's popularity and global reach means it is able to shine a light on everything from human rights abuses to homophobia and environmental concerns.

The 'It Gets Better' project was launched by US journalist Dan Savage in 2010. The YouTube channel tries to prevent suicides among LGBT teenagers by conveying the message that these teens' lives will improve. The channel hosts over 50,000 videos, including many from celebrities, which have been viewed over 50 million times!

There is even a Human Rights Channel on YouTube, launched in 2012, which is a collaboration between the human rights organization WITNESS (www.witness.org) and social media news channel Storyful (www.storyful.com). The channel collects

Protest groups, like this member of the Anonymous, are able to speak directly to the public through videos on YouTube.

together and broadcasts videos shot by real people around the world who find themselves in extraordinary situations – from peace protesters coming under fire from government forces, to families caught up in guerrilla bombings. There are even 'How To' guides on filming protests, while staying safe.

YouTube is in a unique position – part of the mainstream, but also part of the underground. It allows news to be broadcast from countries where foreign journalists are not allowed; places where the real stories are often buried behind government restrictions and banning orders. As an eye on the real world, it is priceless.

Business Matters

Public relations (PR)

This is the practice of conveying messages to the public through the media on behalf of a client. The intention is to change the public's actions by influencing their opinions. For example, to view YouTube not just as an entertainment platform but also as a news delivery service. PR professionals usually target specific sections of the public ('audiences'), since similar opinions tend to be shared by a group of people rather than an entire society.

Brains

Behind The Brand

Danielle Tiedt
Head of Marketing

Tiedt was hired from Microsoft, where she spent 15 years, most recently as general manager of its Bing search engine. Her job was to try and get consumers to use a different search brand, and she oversaw an annual marketing budget of £74m!

At YouTube, Tiedt oversees the branding and promotion of the company's investment in new entertainment channels. It is her job to change users' perception of YouTube from fun web clips to professionally produced TV and movie-quality content.

Head of marketing, Danielle Tiedt, is helping change our views of YouTube.

What does the future hold for YouTube?

What are YouTube's plans for the next five years? Has it reached its peak or can it keep growing? Here we highlight some of the areas that YouTube may focus on to stay ahead of the competition.

We know for sure that YouTube will focus on creating more and more channels, broadcasting to smaller niche markets. Unlike traditional television, where airtime is limited, Internet 'airtime' is infinite. Quantity is just as important as quality, and YouTube relies on its audience choosing what they want to watch.

Advertising methods will need to change to target these niche markets. 'Currently it's one TV commercial run many times,' explains Robert Kyncl. 'It will become 250 video commercials run fewer times but to the right people, using geo-location, age-targeting and interest-targeting.' In other words, YouTube will be able to monitor what you watch, when you watch, how long you watch, and where you watch from – and deliver that information to advertisers, who in turn will show you advertising you actually want to see.

One challenge that YouTube faces is increasing the amount of time that people spend on the site. The average YouTuber currently spends around 5 hours per month on the site – a tiny amount compared to the 5 hours an average person spends watching television per day! If YouTube can persuade people to stay on the site longer, it can sell more advertising, and raise the rates it charges advertisers.

Longer shows would keep visitors on the site, and already there are examples of new shows, like the *Glee/High School Musical*-inspired drama *Side Effects* (produced by Awesomeness TV), running 40-minute episodes. YouTube has also tweaked its video-ranking algorithm to promote clips

Head of content, Robert Kyncl, is behind the successful YouTube Channels.

that keep viewers watching and engaged. So if a video leads to a person clicking on another video and spending more time on the site, it will rank higher.

One thing's for sure – YouTube will be a part of our lives for many years to come.

A group of university students watching YouTube. Will the site begin to rival traditional TV channels over the next 5–10 years?

Business Matters

$

Long-term success

Successful companies are 'market-driven', in other words they focus on satisfying the exact section of the market in which they operate. (All of YouTube's channels target specific markets, however niche.) Successful companies also need to be 'sustainable', meaning that people not only want to use their services now, but that they will continue to want to use them in the future.

YouTube's competitors – and how they measure up

www.metacafe.com
Simply designed site offering music, movies, games, and a variety of channels from Video Game High School to Annoying Orange that are also available on YouTube.

www.Dailymotion.com
Cluttered but very popular site attracting 112 million monthly visitors. Users can open accounts and interact with others.

www.vimeo.com
Stylishly designed site with an active community of users. Charges between £37-£125 per year for video uploads over a certain volume per year.

www.veoh.com
Small but well organized video-sharing site owned by Israeli start-up Qlipso, focuses more on online community than the quality/uniqueness of its videos.

Invent the next YouTube channel!

To create a new product, for example a new YouTube channel, it is helpful to produce a product development brief like the one below. This is a sample brief for a new YouTube channel called Football 24/7.

The SWOT analysis on the page opposite will help you to think about the strengths, weaknesses, opportunities and threats for your product. This can help you to see how feasible and practical your idea is before you think of investing time and money in it.

Product Development Brief

Name of channel: Football 24/7

Type of channel: Bringing the best streamed coverage of football matches from around the world – both new and classic archived games from the last 50 years.

The channel explained (use 25 words or less): Football 24/7 gives you access to the best live football from around the world, with a massive archive of classic matches too!

Target age of users: Users must be 16 and over to subscribe.

What does the channel do?: Football 24/7 allows viewers to access a huge archive of matches from around the world – from live games to classic matches. If you want to watch your heroes – from Diego Maradona to Cristiano Ronaldo – Football 24/7 is the one-stop channel for all football fans.

Are there any similar products already available?: None that we are aware of.

What makes your brand different?: Sky and BT offer Premier League and international live games, but no channel offers such a range of classic matches from around the world to enjoy in full at any time.

SWOT Analysis
(Strengths, Weaknesses, Opportunities and Threats)

Name of YouTube channel you are assessing ...
Football 24/7

The table below will help you assess your YouTube channel. By addressing all four areas, you can make your product stronger and more likely to be a success.

Questions to consider

Strengths Does your channel offer something unique? Is there anything innovative about it? What are its USPs (unique selling points)? Why will people use this channel instead of a similar one?	There are no other channels currently available offering the same service. Football 24/7's USP is that it's the only place you can stream full matches from around the world from the last 50 years.
Weaknesses Why wouldn't people use this channel? Can everyone use it? Does it does everything it says it can?	Football 24/7 is only of interest to football fans. Plus it will mostly appeal to older fans, who want to reminisce over games they might have seen, or heard about from many years ago. Users have to be over 16 to subscribe to the channel. At first the archive of older games will be limited, but more will come online all the time, as licensing deals are signed with international broadcasters for their archives
Opportunities Will the area that the channel serves become more important over time? Can the channel be improved in the future, e.g. adapted for other uses? Can it be used globally? Can it develop new USPs?	We predict that around the time of big tournaments, e.g. World Cups and European Championships, the demand for the channel will increase. If the channel is a success, it could be expanded to cover other sports, e.g. American football and Cricket. The channel could also expand to include interviews and programmes about classic players.
Threats Is the market that you are selling into shrinking? Will it face competition from other channels? Are any of your weaknesses so bad they might affect the channel in the long run?	The popularity of football worldwide is increasing – no danger of the market reducing. Other broadcasters with large archives of their own, e.g. the BBC and Sky, may not licence content to Football 24/7 and decide to launch their own channels instead. We believe that the opportunities to generate revenue from advertising on the clips will persuade content providers to licence us their content.

Do you have what it takes to work at YouTube?
Try this quiz!

1) You're going to a friend's birthday party tonight. Do you:

a) Worry about what to buy her for a present. Then stick a tenner in an envelope.

b) Remind yourself to take some pictures to post on Facebook afterwards.

c) Video everything – from getting ready to the moment she blows out the candles – and post it for all your friends!

2) You have a presentation to do at school. Do you:

a) Find out what your best friend's writing about and do the same thing.

b) Spend a couple of nights on it, then print out some pictures from the Internet to liven it up.

c) Edit a video of clips you have found online.

3) You want to learn the guitar. Do you:

a) Buy a book of 'Easy Beatles songs' – then give up after page 10.

b) Go to a guitar teacher for a few weeks, but stop because you can't afford the cost of lessons any more.

c) Teach yourself from videos. There are some amazing teachers online, and all free!

4) What do you want to do when you leave school?

a) I'm hoping to work for my dad. Then I can be late for work, and he won't sack me.

b) University first. Then a job in banking.

c) I want to study computer science, then get a job with a start-up. I love social media!

5) Your hero is:

a) Jack Whitehall – a great stand-up comedian.

b) Nelson Mandela – led South Africa out of apartheird.

c) Chad Hurley – founder of YouTube.

6) You have the chance to meet one YouTuber. Who would it be?

a) Charlie –from 'Charlie bit my finger – again!'

b) PSY from *Gangnam Style* – I want to learn his dance moves.

c) Jamal Edwards – the opportunity to get any tips from him would be amazing!

7) You have the opportunity to launch your own YouTube channel. Do you:

a) Ask a few friends for ideas… and then forget about it.

b) Launch a channel with videos of your cat sleeping. Then be disappointed when it only gets 20 views.

c) Choose a subject that you really enjoy. And most importantly, be original, be funny, and upload regularly!

Results

Mostly As: Sorry, but your chance of working at YouTube is looking shaky! It doesn't sound like you have the interest in video streaming or social media to succeed at this world-famous company.

Mostly Bs: You are thoughtful and hard-working, but you need to put more effort into standing out from the pack if you want to succeed in a very competitive business.

Mostly Cs: Congratulations, it sounds like you have what it takes to succeed at YouTube. Keep working hard at school, and pushing to be the best, and who knows?

Glossary

algorithm a set of mathematical instructions that a computer uses to help calculate an answer or mathematical problem

bandwidth a measurement of the amount of information that can be sent between computers through a phone line

brainchild an original idea, plan or object that someone has invented

brainstorming meeting to suggest new ideas for possible development

censor to remove anything offensive from books, films and so on

copyright holder the person or organization who holds the legal right to control the production, distribution or selling of a film, photograph, piece of music or similar

eucalyptus a type of tree

harness to control something (in order to use its power)

homophobia a fear or dislike of gay people

LBGT lesbian, gay, bisexual and transgender

lucrative producing a lot of money

mainstream considered normal by most people

monetize to convert something into a form of currency

niche market a small area of trade within the economy, usually involving specialist interests

perception a belief or opinion, often held by many people

phenomenal extremely successful, especially in a surprising way

post upload to the Internet

scale to increase the size and importance of a company

streaming sending audio or video to a computer or mobile phone directly from the Internet, so that it doesn't need to be downloaded and saved first

tailor to make something specially, so that it is right for a particular person or group

unique unusual, or one of a kind

venture capital money lent to someone to start a new business, especially one that involves risks and will make large profits if successful

viral becoming popular very quickly through communication from one person to another on the Internet

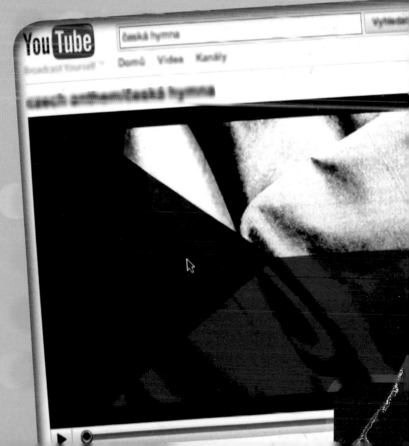

Index